NUMBRILUGU

THE NUMBER STORY

SMALL BOOK ONE

ENGLISH – ESTONIAN

*Numbers Teach Children
Their Number Names*

written and illustrated by

MISS ANNA

Early Reader Edition of *The Number Story 1*
Bronze Medal Winner, 2016 Wishing Shelf Book Award

Library of Congress Control Number: 2018902040

Names: Miss Anna, author.
Title: Number story : numbers teach children their number names / Miss Anna.
Description: Portland, OR: Lumpy Publishing, 2018.
Identifiers: ISBN 978-1-945977-50-3 | LCCN 2018902040
Summary: The pictures and rhymes present stories which introduce numbers 0-10.
Subjects: LCSH Numeration—English--Estonian--Pictorial works--Juvenile literature. | BISAC JUVENILE NONFICTION /
Languages: English--Estonian
Classification: LCC QA141.3 .M57 2018 | DDC 513—dc23

Publisher: Lumpy Publishing
Website: www.missannabooks.com
Email: missanna@missannabooks.com

Paperback: ISBN 978-1-945977-50-3
Printed in the U.S.A.   1 3 5 7 9 10 8 6 4 2

Tahate õppida meie numbrite nimesi?

It is very easy and a lot of fun!

See on väga lihtne ja lõbus!

Say-along our little jingle

Laula kaasa meie laulukest.

starting from Number One!

Alustame number ühest!

1

ONE   looks like my one finger.

ÜKS

Näeb välja nagu sõrm.

ONE!
ÜKS!

2

TWO trails a tail.

KAKS

Talle meeldib saba.

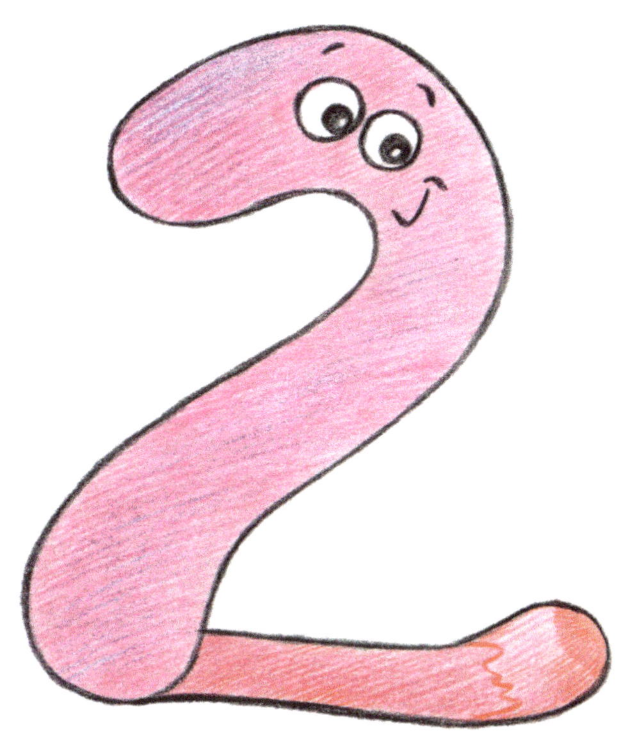

A TAIL! SABA!

3

THREE has bumps.

KOLM

Tal on künkad.

BUMPY!   KÜNKAD!

4

FOUR carries a sail.

NELI

On purjepaat.

4
A SAIL!
PURJEPAAT!
PURJEKOMPLEKT!

5

FIVE   is a racing track.

VIIS

Näeb välja nagu rallirada.

VROOM
VROOOM!
VROOOM!
1

SIX curves like a snail.

KUUS

Kõverdub nagu tigu.

A SNAIL! TIGU!

7

S E V E N has a sharp angle.

SEITSE

Tal on terav nurk.

OUCH!
AII!

8

KAHEKSA

Tal on Ameerika mäed.

rollercoaster

JUHHEI!
YIPPEE!

NINE   is a bubble on a stick.

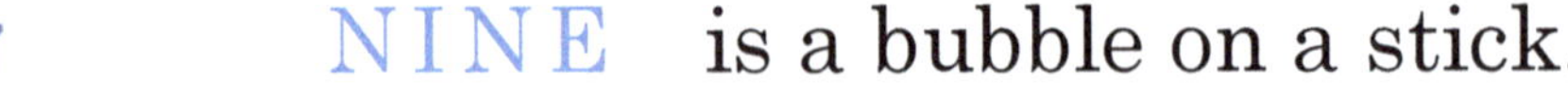

ÜHEKSA

On seebimull.

A BUBBLE! MULL!

10

TEN   is an eye of a whale.

KÜMME

See on vaala silm.

PLAKS, PLAKS!
WINK!
HELLO! HALLOO!

And
JAA

0

ZERO   is an empty pail.

NULL

Ta on tühi tünn.

IT'S
EMPTY!
See on tühi!

Thank you for playing with us today.

We had a lot of fun too!

Aitäh, et mängisid täna meiega.

Meil oli väga lõbus!

We are your Number friends,
Zero to Ten,
Who will be here for you~
Me oleme sinu Numbrisõbrad
Ühest Kümneni!
Me oleme alati sinu jaoks olemas~

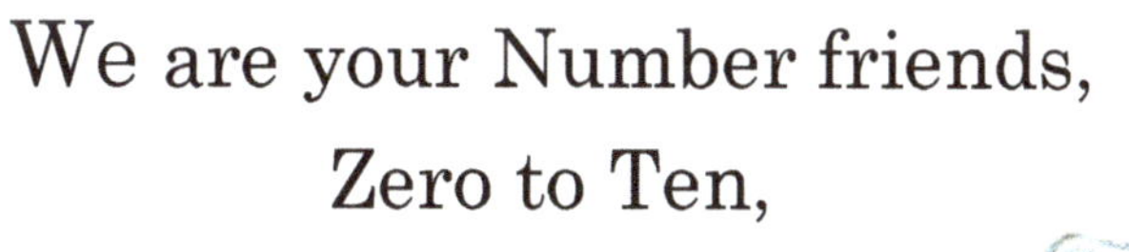

Bye-bye now!
See you again soon!
Tšau-tšau!
Näeme varsti jälle!

The Numbers are *SINGING* too!

To sing-a-long, look for Miss Anna Number Story
at your favorite music store like iTUNES.

MP3

Numbers 0-10
IDENTIFYING
& COUNTING

Numbers 11-20
& Ordinals
first, second, third...

Numbers 0-100
& Place Values
ones, tens, hundreds...

About Clocks
& Telling Time
hours, minutes, second

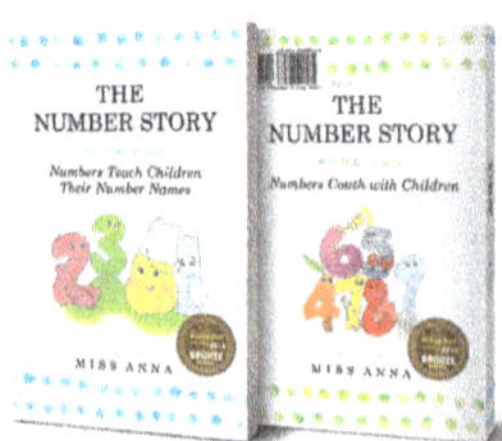

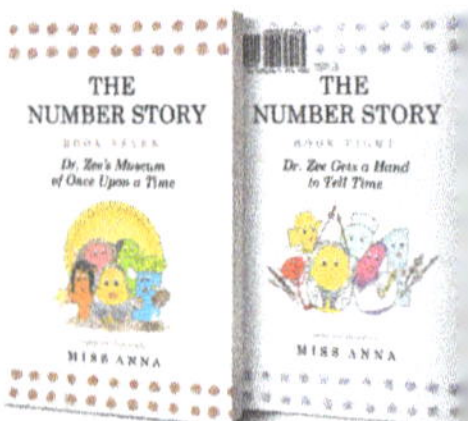

Number Story 1 & 2
isbn: 978-0-996216-48-7

Number Story 3 & 4
isbn: 978-1-945977-01-5

Number Story 5 & 6
isbn: 978-1-945977-06-0

Number Story 7 & 8
isbn: 978-1-949320-40-

For more Miss Anna books to love,
visit us at

w w w . m i s s a n n a b o o k s . c o m

Numbers are working hard all over the world!
Come Travel the World with Us!

www.ingramcontent.com/pod-product-compliance
Lightning Source LLC
Chambersburg PA
CBHW041101050726
47599CB00018B/2224